Tech Research
Phrase Book

By:

Susan Louise Peterson

Tech Research Phrase Book

Susan Louise Peterson

CONTENTS

PREFACE

Most people working in the professional world are aware that the technology field has changed the way reports are written. Those in the academic field are extremely aware of how the technology world was the changed the focus of grant proposals, research projects and in particular the way a thesis or dissertation is written. Including technological phrases in these reports adds a sense of knowledge about the ever changing digital and technological changes taking place. These technological phrases can be incorporated to discuss the focus of a project as well as the objectives, evaluation, assessment and investigation components that are featured in the study. As well, the technological phrases can be added to explain the results or make recommendations for the study. The technological change phrases in the ***Tech Research Phrase Book*** provide an added bonus of building on future technological change and writing about these future perspectives.

PROLOGUE

The Tech Research Phrase Book invites readers to explore how technological terms and phrases can be brainstormed into a traditional writing framework. The book provides an abundance of opportunities to develop a sense of academic and professional writing with technological prompts and starters. Many of these technological phrases are geared toward beginning a project or research proposal by establishing a focus with objectives and then moving into the evaluation and assessment components. As with many written projects the technological phrases are fused with the investigator guidelines, results, recommendations and ability to address technological change for present and future issues.

ACKNOWLEDGEMENTS

I want to thank my past professors who gave me so many writing tips and suggestions to fine tune my writing of academic papers. Each little phrase and alternative writing suggestion helped me rethink my writing style and thought process for using written words.

I want to thank my husband whose 'tech support' is invaluable as I deal with websites, manuscripts and promotional materials. His unbending support never wavers. I also wanted to thank my beautiful twin daughters who each have their own definite personality and goals. I wish my girls the best in their journey to find peace and happiness along with a few (temporary) bumps in the road.

INTRODUCTION

Many academic writers and students lose focus and have trouble keeping track of both the research writing principles and the technology elements of a written project. In the ***Tech Research Phrase Book,*** writers can jumpstart their proposals by seeing a variety of technological phrases that can be incorporated in grant or proposal development and then discuss the futuristic possibilities related to technological change. As an academic writer, phrases are important in helping combat writer's block and then helping the writer have a starting point that can be used to build the specific and personal angles and challenges of a particular study or investigation. The aim of the ***Tech Research Phrase Book*** is to integrate 'tech' phrases into writing proposals with a fast paced focus that may incorporate many new and changing technological issues.

CHAPTER 1

TECHNOLOGICAL FOCUS PHRASES

the educational technological plan focused on

the focus of the technological mission is to

the technological vision and focus supported the

the technological targets focused on the area of

the technological programming focused on

the technological benchmarks were the focus of

technological quality was a focal point for the

the technological development was one focus

the technological framework focused on the

each technological strand had a focus

the technological team focused the project on

technological administrators were the focus of the project

technological theory was part of the focus

the technological research project focused on two main areas

the integrated technological projects was a major focus

technological trends were a primary focus

technological outcomes were focused on

technological course evaluation was a central focus

technological assessment focused on the areas of

technological funding was focused on the current budget

technological controversies became the focus

technological priorities focused around the

the technological setting was the focus of the research

technological improvement was the grant focus

the technological bill focused the funding on

technological outreach focused on programs to improve the

the technological management clearly focused on

the technological goals of the study focused around

the technological objectives were a big focus of the study

the technological units were a focal point for

the technological resources were part of the organizational focus

the technological guidance focused on involving

the technological assignment was focused on skill development to

the technological policy was a focus of the mini research project

the technological preparation focus added to the research

the technological paradigm focused on

the technological measurement was only a small focus of

the technological scholars focused on the topic of

the technological reform was focused on change

the technological productivity was only part of the research focus

the technological spending became a big focus concern

a technological endowment was designed to focus on

a technological certification was focused on skill improvement

a technological context was used to focus on

technological inservice education was focused on training the

technological delivery was the focus of the problem area

technological foundations focused the project toward

a technological philosophy was focused toward

the technological arena presentations were focused on

the technological field focused on job creation

the technological implications focused on a common theme

the technological practicum was first focused on

the technological focus was complex

the technological advocate focused the researchers to a common theme

the technological level focused on

the technological staff abilities became a new focus

the technological endorsement of the university focused on

the technological services focused toward

technological mentors focused assistance to

technological challenges were focused in a new direction

technological incentives helped focus the research subjects on

technological tutorials focused support on

technological organizations supported the focus

the technological presentation focused on key points

technological steps focused in two directions

a technological internship focused on improving the

the technological system was a focus of the grant

technological testing focused on skills of the presentation

a technological competition helped focus on top projects

the technological market focused on an upward trend

the technological board was split in their focus

the technological critique focused on ways to improve

technological terminology was focused on

technological commentary focused toward the issue

technological requirements were focused toward the regulations

technological regions focused on different aspects

there was a strong technological contention focused on the disagreements

technological education was focused on the skills

technology focused on providing an enriching education to

the technological stipend focused on purchasing new materials

the technological essentials had a curriculum focus

technological extension was adapted with an outreach focus

technological enrichment was focused at the end of the program

technological development was part of the grant focus

technological organization focused on a team approach

technological specialists were part of the focus

technological planning was focused on business development

the technological goals had a learning focus

a technological guide was adapted with an educational focus

a technological integrated focus was provided

technological requirements focused on legal issues

technological activities focused on group research participation

the technological focus was a slow developing process

the technological curriculum was poorly developed

a technological workshop focused on data collection

the technological revision focused on research paper corrections

a technological blueprint focused on equipment challenges

the technological project had a historical research focus

the technological committee focused on the researcher's qualifications

the technological coordinator focused on developing a research team to

the technological trends were focused on changing equipment needs

the technological implications focused on program development

the technological priorities focused on the school district's mission to

the evolving curriculum focused on technological issues

the technological approach had a training focus

the technological components had a two-fold focus

the technological framework was geared toward a research focus

the technological design focused on energy efficiency

the technological evaluation had a research design focus

the technological foundation had a fundraising focus

the technology strands were focused on the research samples

the technology focus was adapted to the curriculum

the technology core had a learning focus

the technology overview focused on the weaknesses of the project

the technology grant focused on elementary schools

the comprehensive technology plan focused on broad research issues

the technological sequence focused on four structured steps

the technological workshops focused on administering the

the innovative technological approach focused on new computers

the technology in-service research project focused on

the technology center focused on extension and outreach

the technology instruction was focused on training researchers

the technology content had a design focus

the technology curriculum focused on three areas

the technology vitae was the focus of the researcher's qualifications

the technology budget focused on overspending

the technology grant focused on the project's strengths

the technology courses had a blended focus

the technology preparation courses focused on well trained leaders

the technology curriculum had an internet focus

the technological assessment was focused on test administration

the technology focused the research project toward

the ongoing technology issues focused on resolving complaints

the technology emphasis focused on storage issues

the technology transformation focused on new equipment

the technology linkages focused on connecting two research projects

the technology decisions were based on the purpose of the study

the technology recommendations focused on subject participation a new technological approach focused on

the technological analysis focused on problem areas

the technological specialist focused the research towards

a progressive technological plan focused on recent changes

the technology offerings had a limited focus

the prescribed technology guidelines limited the research

the technological improvement came from a focused research study

the technological analysis was research focused

the long range technology plan was not research focused

a differentiated technology curriculum focused on various learning styles

a thematic technology plan focused on

the multidisciplinary technology plan focused on building the department

the technology rules focused on state guidelines

the basic technology plan had a long term focus

the adapted technology plan focused forward

technology journal writing was focused on

technology writing examples provided the focus

shared technology writing experiences focused on

revised technology writings were focused on clarification

structured technology writing helped focus on mistakes

technology writing logs focused the project toward

the technological writing format was focused on

the technological writings were revised to focus on

the technological dialogue focused on

the technology paragraph focused the direction of the study

the technology publications had a single focus

the technology situation streamed to focus towards a

the technology topics had a student focus

the technology format focused around the

the final stage of the technology plan focused on

the technology objectives focused in the area of

a balanced technology program focuses on

the context of the technology plan was focused on

the technology tools had an instructional focus

the independent technology writings were focused on

the technology tasks focused around

the technology pre-writing task focused on

the technology solutions were focused around the researcher's
questions

the revised technology plans had a fresh focus

rewriting the technology plan presented a new focus

the technology instructions had a very detailed focus

the technological questions focused on

the technological draft focused around

a technological suggestion was focused on

the technology plan focused on small pieces of the project

the technology plan focused on article submissions

the technological criteria focused on department needs

the technological discrepancies focused on errors

the technology focus was presented in a narrative

the technology survey focused on

the technology outcomes were not related to the focus of

the technology benefits were an important focus of

the technology focus was compared to

the technological ideas were not related to the focus

the technological strategies had a meaningful focus

the technology experiments were computer focused

technology skills were a strong focus of the project

technology usage was an important focus of

the focus of the technology rules centered around

the technology function was part of the focus

specialized technology projects were focused on

CHAPTER 2

TECHNOLOGICAL OBJECTIVE PHRASES

technology objective related content

technology objective related activities

measureable technology objectives

functional level technology objectives

technology objectives were developed

conditional technology objectives

competency based technology objectives

specific technology objectives

practical technology objectives

general technology objectives

stated technology objectives

instructional technology objectives

educational technology objectives

key technology objectives

competency stated technological objectives

technology case study objectives

terminal technology objectives

major technology objectives

contemporary technology objectives

objective technology components

objective technology requirements

listed technology objectives

objective technology examples

standard technology objectives

objective technological statements

highlighted technological objectives

featured technological objectives

meaningful technological objectives

planned technology objectives

proposed technology objectives

reinforced technology objectives

specific technology objectives

designed technology objectives

written technology objectives

technology objective clarification

revised technology objectives

objective technological strands

technological course objectives

technology level objectives

topic objectives related to technology

focused technology objectives

research technology objectives

teaching technology objectives

formulated technology objectives

program technology objectives

seminar technology objectives

objective technological statements

objective technological content

achievable technology objectives

relevant technology objectives

observable technology objectives

strategic technology objectives

identified technology objectives

technology objective development

meeting technology objectives

objective technology options

developed technology objectives

changing technology objectives

objective technology terminology

objective technology definition

redundant technology objectives

graduate technology objectives

clarifying technology objective

technological philosophy objective

technological evaluation objectives

confusing technological objectives

detailed technological objectives

prioritized technological objectives

content technological objectives

organized technological objectives

flexible technological objectives

evolving technological objectives

problem solving technological objectives

cultural technological objectives

multifaceted technological objectives

technology objectives were modified to

technology objective outcomes

defined technology objectives

inflexible technology objectives

the technology objectives were rearranged

technology orientation objectives were developed

extra resources were need to address the technology objectives

technology objectives were perceived as

a production team helped with the technology objectives

the primary technology objective was to

technological objectives were compiled into

the technological objectives were applied to specific departments

technological objectives can be shaped into

technological objectives were made in phrases

technological objectives can be planned in stages

regulations had to be followed in writing the technological objectives

a supervisor reviewed the technological objectives

the technology objectives were requested by

a cohort supervised the technology objective development

writing the technological objectives was difficult

a model was used to demonstrate the technology objectives

technological objectives were prevalent in the study

an abundance of sources were utilized in developing the technological objectives

a sketch was useful in showing the technological objectives

a tentative report was made on the technology objectives

a check-off list was completed on the technology objectives

technological objectives eliminated the need for

technological objectives were denoted with

a security check was made on the technological objectives

technology objectives were matched to the inventory

extra material was needed for the technology objectives

the technology objectives were meaningful for the study

there was a meeting to discuss technological objectives

the media reviewed the technological objectives

the press was interested in the technological objectives

technology objectives were routine

the procedure to pick the technology objectives was explained to

specific techniques were used for the technological objectives

technology objectives were needed in the

technology objectives were misunderstood by

the technology objectives were confusing

a major technological objective came from

the technology objectives were insufficient

students gained new skills from the technology objectives

technology objectives were paramount to

it was necessary to make the technological changes clear

technology objectives were made without prior approval

a prerequisite for the technology objective was

technology objectives were urgently needed

technology objectives were developed quickly

technology objectives were ranked in importance

each technology objective was carefully evaluated

ongoing reviews were made on the technology objectives

there was a technology classroom management objective

multiage technology objective

classroom management was a technology objective

one technology objective involved rotating classrooms

a technology classroom routine objective

technology training objective

technology practicum objective

technology behavior objective

technology examination objective

technology internship objective

technology procedures objective

technology laboratory objective

technology plan objective

model technology objective

technological privileges were not part of the objective

technological survey objective

technological medication objective

technological event objective

injuries were addressed in the technological objective

technological design objective

an alternative objective was developed to address technology needs

the technology inventory objective was designed to

technology alternatives objective

technology inventory objective

technology checklist objective

the objective of the technology center was to

technology workstation objective

technology newsletter objective

technology curriculum objective

technology activity objective

technology discussion objective

technology volunteer objective

technology homework objective

the objective of the technology trip was to

the objective of the technology assignment was to

the technology seatwork objective was

the technology vocabulary development objective involved

the technology workshop objective included

the technology partnership objectives involved many organizations

technological difficulties were not addressed in the objectives

technological task objective

technological file storage objective

technological strength objective

technological enrollment objective

technology attendance objective

technology demonstration objective

technology equipment objective

technology classroom conduct objective

technology distractions were not addressed in the objective

technology exhibit objective

technology representative objective

technology delegation objective

technology publication objective

technology objectives were developed for each location

a technology objective was developed to address a unique situation

each technological objective had a standard

objective technology funds were used to

technology conference objective

cutbacks were addressed in the technology objective

a technology equipment arrangement objective

a technology format objective

technological supplement objective

technology celebration objective

technology announcement objective

technology classroom objective

an objective was designed with technology rewards and incentives

technology testing objective

technology methods objective

technology relocation was included in the objective

technology restructuring objective

technology objectives included

CHAPTER 3

TECHNOLOGICAL EVALUATION PHRASES

the technology self evaluation was presented to

parents were asked to complete a technological evaluation

a technological evaluation unit was developed

a technological evaluation was used by the researchers to

the technological evaluation methods were

the evaluation questions were technological in nature

a written technological evaluation was used

the technological program received a negative evaluation

the evaluation process included technology components

an objective technological evaluation was developed

a summative technological evaluation was used to

the technology performance evaluation included looking at

the technology evaluation design was incorporated to

technology program evaluators helped inspect the project

a technology course evaluation was created

evaluation outcomes had many technology features

a critical technological evaluation was used

a comprehensive technological evaluation was developed

the technological evaluation was completed quickly

a rated technological evaluation was included

an informal technological evaluation provided valuable information for

the formal technological evaluation was very helpful

the technological evaluation criteria was confusing

the technological evaluation methodology was sequenced

the technological evaluation practices were approved by the board

the technological evaluation theory was included in the proposal

the technological operation evaluation was very involved

the technological evaluation tools were listed in the program

the technological evaluation plans were sent to the research committee

the technological evaluation issues were limited to

a technological evaluation consultant was used

the technological evaluation report revealed that

the annual technological evaluation was presented to

the technological evaluation portion of the project revealed

a technological evaluation period was helpful for

a formative technological evaluation was included

the technological evaluation documentation concluded

the technological evaluation discussions were useful for

the technological evaluation conference was formed to

technological evaluative instruments helped analyze equipment needs

periodic technological evaluations were necessary to

technology evaluation techniques had to be developed to

ongoing technological evaluations were used throughout

educational technological evaluations had to be developed to

the technological evaluation component was a big part of the project

the technology evaluation trends leaned towards

the technological evaluation orientation was needed for the staff to

the technology evaluation summary helped put the project in perspective for

the technology evaluation timeline was extremely helpful for

the technology evaluation team was formed to

the technology evaluation presentation was a helpful support

the technological evaluation checklist was needed to

the technological evaluation checkpoints were used to

a technological evaluation folder was placed in the office for

an alternative technological evaluation was used for

a technological evaluation calendar was printed to

the technological evaluation information included

technological evaluation handouts were given to staff members

the technological evaluation responsibilities included

a computerized technological evaluation was used to

the technological evaluation guidelines helped clarify

technology group evaluations proved to be helpful

a multifaceted technological evaluation was developed to

the technological evaluation materials included

prior technological evaluations were reviewed

a confidential technological evaluation was used

a technological course evaluation was left out

routine technological evaluations were used throughout the year

yearly technological evaluations were completed

the technology evaluation questions were confusing

a standard technology evaluation was used as a guideline for

an oral technological evaluation was ineffective

the revised technological evaluation was much improved

the technological evaluation results included

an established technological evaluation was used to

a uniform technological evaluation proved helpful

a questionable technological evaluation was used

technological evaluator training was held to

the graded technological evaluation was impressive

a more suitable technological evaluation was chosen to

technological evaluations were made on an experimental basis

a tentative plan was made for the technological evaluation

experts were invited to comment on the technological evaluation

explanations were developed to clarify the technology evaluation

a brief note outlined the technological evaluation

there was a budget summary for the technological evaluation

technological evaluation provided opportunities to search for

students completed the technological evaluations

remarks were made on the technology evaluations

a highlight of the technological evaluation was

a key point of the technological evaluation was

technological evaluations were checked by

the staff articulated the need for technological evaluations

an extension of the technology evaluation was developed

an extra benefit of the technology evaluation was

the technology evaluation helped facilitate

the technology evaluation was frustrating for

teachers were familiarized with the technological evaluation

the main feature of the technology evaluation is

a file was kept with the technology evaluations

technological evaluations were finalized

technological evaluations are being completed by

flexibility was required for completing the technology evaluations

predictions were made regarding the technology evaluation

a technology evaluation forecast was developed

the strength of the technological evaluation was

the justification for the technological evaluation is based on

a technological evaluation was used to fulfill the

a functional part of the technological evaluation was

technological evaluations are fundamental for

technological evaluations were grouped for

a council explained the technology evaluations

a generous donation provided the funds for the technology evaluation

the merit of the technological evaluation centered around

gradually a technological evaluation was developed

the technology evaluation was welcomed

there was growth and expansion from the technology evaluation

leadership was needed to explain the technology evaluations

the school was a pioneer for developing the technology evaluation

the technological evaluation was terminated due to

a guidebook was helpful in making the technological evaluations

technological evaluations were accompanied by

problems were uncovered in the technological evaluations

the philosophy behind the technological evaluation was

technological evaluations were valuable for

an essential part of the technology evaluation was

the technological evaluation results were far reaching

there was a link between the technological evaluations and

technological evaluations were connected with

a crucial part of the technological evaluation was

some of the technology evaluations were unrealistic

changes in the technology program came from evaluations

the technological evaluation advanced the

the evaluation helped refine the technology

a shortcoming for the technological evaluation was

funds for the technology evaluations were depleted

an abbreviated technological evaluation was used to

technological evaluations were made in conjunction with

technology evaluations are currently being considered

staff will meet with the board members on the technology
evaluation

schools were obligated to implement the technology evaluation

departments worked independently on the technology evaluations

technology evaluations were made systematically

technology evaluations were personalized to the needs of

a fundamental part of the technology evaluation was

technological evaluations were an inevitable part of

the board was convinced to complete the technology evaluations

departments showed evidence for the need of technology evaluations

technology evaluations were confirmed by

there was a probe into the technology evaluations

technology evaluations varied among departments

directives were given for the technology evaluations

the technological evaluations had an international focus

there were interruptions in developing the technology evaluations

technology evaluations were first introduced by

each technology evaluation was researched by

technology evaluations were executed by

the most productive technology evaluation included

staff were not involved in the technology evaluation

technology evaluation problems were examined

students were excited about the technology evaluation

technology evaluations were intertwined with

further recommendations were made on the technology evaluations

the conclusion of the technology evaluation report was

teachers explored the additional technological evaluation

technology evaluations involved an expedition of

there was a delay in starting the technological evaluations

technology evaluations were well planned

there was a need for a technology evaluation

the technology evaluation provided a vast amount of information

a layout of the technology evaluation included

the administration took the lead in the technology evaluation

teachers presented lectures on the technology evaluations

lessons focused on the technology evaluations

technology evaluations were verified by

a memo stated the technology evaluation was being distributed

professors made suggestions on the technology evaluation

technology evaluations were restricted to

a bulletin outlined the technology evaluation

technology evaluations were presented on video

technology changes were fashioned after

technology evaluations occurred daily

the main technology evaluation was

specialized training was provided for the technological evaluation

the web research technological evaluation survey included

the technological evaluations varied in their content

the steps in completing the technological evaluation were

the main purpose of the technology evaluation was

the technology evaluation draft was a fluent document

the language in the technology evaluation was confusing

the technology evaluation was part of an experiment

each technology evaluation experiment was diverse

the technology evaluation was patterned after

the technology evaluation was amended to include

the technology evaluation was suitable for

the technology evaluation included information on performance goals

the technology evaluation specified the need for

the technology evaluation terminology was difficult to understand

each technology evaluation included detailed information

the technology evaluation had scholarly components

each technology evaluation contained relevant information

the technology evaluation was translated into foreign languages

the technology evaluation experience was hindered by

the technology evaluation was integrated with

CHAPTER 4

TECHNOLOGICAL ASSESSMENT PHRASES

technology assessment portfolio

technology cyclical assessment

technological assessment process

technology assessment information

multiple technology assessments

technology self assessment

technology assessment tool

structured technology assessment

technology assessment responsibilities

consistent technology assessments were used to

technology assessment folder

alternative technology assessment

technological assessment practice

the technology assessment facilitator

computerized technological assessment

group technology assessments were used to

ongoing technology assessments

the technology assessment procedure included

the technology assessment results were presented

an internal technology assessment was used to

the technology assessment instrument developed from

prior technology assessments revealed that

technology assessment techniques

technology assessment guidelines

technology assessment journals

technology assessment meetings were held at the

the technology assessment method involved using

a multifaceted technology assessment was designed to

a national technological assessment was developed

the technological assessment calendar was posted for

technological assessment materials were distributed to

there were technology assessment problems

the technology assessment report revealed

a confidential technology assessment was used to

informal technology assessments

subjective technology assessments

systematic technology assessments

formal technology assessments

technology assessment summation

technology writing assessment

extensive technology assessment

technology assessment directions

upcoming technology assessment

adequate technology assessment

technology assessment model

technology needs assessment

oral technology assessment

technology assessment coordinator

original technology assessment

initial technology assessment

technology assessment resources

technology assessment outline

technology assessment framework

technology assessment document

technology assessment plan

technology assessment strategy

technology assessment scope

preliminary technology assessment

technology assessment draft

technology assessment sequence

technology assessment chart

technology assessment layout

the proposed technology assessment included

additional technology assessments

technology assessment expertise

the technology assessment was deemed effective

a functional technology assessment was used to

the revised technology assessment

decisive technology assessment

technology assessment standards

technology assessment recommendations

technology assessment notification

technology assessment questions

technology assessment examination

technology assessment survey

comprehensive technology assessments

reasonable technology assessment

amended technology assessment

reliable technology assessments

technology assessment narrative

technology assessment review

technology assessment critique

technology assessment development

technology assessment concepts

professional technology assessments

technology assessment cases

technology assessment development project

technology assessment stages

the technology assessments were divided by age

the technology assessments were developed as needed

the technology assessments took a developmental approach

a linguistic technology assessment was compiled

a technology assessment was provided for

the technology assessment assumptions were

technology assessments had a language component

technology assessment areas

technology assessment studies

technology assessment was related to

the technology assessment process involved

technology assessment issues varied

technology assessments took into concern the motor skills of

technology assessment period

technology assessments covered a wide range of topics

technology assessment strategies

technology assessment influences came from

technology assessment factors varied greatly in the project

technology assessment was helpful for decision making

symbolic technology assessment

technology assessment experiences

technology assessment was part of academic development

technology assessment environment

cultural technology assessment

optimal technology assessment

technology assessment aspects

technology assessment questions

technology assessment contributions

early technology assessment development included

technology assessment limitations

technology assessment expectations

technology assessment overview

technology assessment problems

technology assessment growth

technology assessment adjustment

technology assessment sequence

technology assessment policy issues

technology assessment policy initiatives

technology assessment collaboration

technology assessment perspectives

public technology assessment policy

developing policies for technology assessments

technology assessment policy making

technology assessment board policy

technology assessment academic policies

technology assessment regulations

technology assessment notification

implement effective technology assessments

technology assessment policy decisions

technology assessment records

technology assessment planning conference

formulating technology assessment policies

future technology assessments

technology assessment analysis

technology assessment research

departmental technology assessment policies

technology assessment staff

technology assessment monitoring

establishing technology assessment policy

technology assessment linkages

changing technology assessment policies

technology assessment dimensions

appropriate technology assessment

technology assessment observations

technology assessment characteristics

technology assessment practices

technology assessment research

staff technology assessment development

technology assessment skill development

technology assessment development articles

technology assessment patterns

technology assessment milestones

technology assessment changes

technology assessment interest

technology assessment theory

technology assessment topics

maintaining technology assessment policies

technology assessment policy review

technology assessment policy guidelines

technology assessment policy standards

consistent technology assessment

recognized technology assessment policy

technology assessment policy violations

technology assessment policy impact

technology assessment policies were needed to

corresponding technology assessment policies

technology assessment targets

technology assessment documentation

correlating technology assessment

technology assessment timelines

connected technology assessment policies

adequate technology assessment

managed technology assessment policies

technology assessment administration

required technology assessment policies

technology assessment policy announcement

technology assessment angles

technology assessment applied policies

technology assessment revitalization

technology assessment attached policy

generated technology assessment policy

sufficient technology assessment policies

technology assessment approach

technology assessment choices

technology assessment classification

technology assessment chart

technology assessment collective policies

the demands of the technology assessment included

the technology assessment description included

working technology assessment policy included

the technology assessment sample policy indicated

technology assessment professionals

technology assessment comparative policies

global technology assessment

technology assessment problem areas

technology assessment resolutions

technology assessment alternatives

technology assessment compliance

technology assessment knowledge

technology assessment terms

technology assessment progressive policies

technology assessment regulatory policies

technology assessment accountability

technology assessment disputes were solved by

internal technology assessment policy

technology assessment efforts

CHAPTER 5

TECHNOLOGICAL INVESTIGATION PHRASES

a technological investigation was conducted to

technological research investigation evidence

the proficiency of the technological research investigation was

a technological investigation was completed in

a technology design investigation was used to

a research appointment was made in the technology design staff

the technology investigation experience was interrupted by

technology investigation support was provided by

a technology investigation record was kept

technology investigation research funding was needed

technology investigation grant proposals were presented to

a technology investigation fellowship was developed

the technology investigation background was important for

a scholarly technology investigation was needed to

technology investigation publications were provided to

professors were invited to the technology investigation program

a technology investigation committee was formed to

conducting technology investigations was left to the

there was a combined technology investigation commitment

the technology investigation agenda included

technological investigation excellence was encouraged

the philosophy of the technological investigation centered around

department resources were utilized for the technology
investigation

a technological investigation research team was developed to

the technological investigation environment was confusing

the technology investigation responsibilities were posted

the technology investigation applications were created to

a technology investigation partnership was formed with

the technology investigation expectations were

the technology investigation organization helped to

technological investigation scholarship was encouraged

a technological investigation collaboration was formed between
departments

technology investigation studies was part of the program

technological investigation research time was given to professors for

solid technological investigations revealed

technological investigation strengths were noted

the technological investigation expertise was broad

technological investigation skills were needed for

technological investigation proposals were invited for submission

technology investigation research ethics were

the technological investigation needed credibility

technology investigation interest was high

technology investigation research methods

technology investigation research population

technology investigation research ability was limited

technology investigation strategies

a technology investigation research advisor was used to

the technology investigation goals were

the potential of the technology investigation was centered around

a long term technological investigation

technology investigation innovation

technology investigation preparation included

basic technology investigation techniques

a technological investigation research approach

the technology investigation was published

technology investigations techniques included

technology investigation research areas

technological investigation writing

the technology investigation track involved

a technological investigation presentation helped to explain

technological investigation research evidence

it was an extensive technological investigation

the technology investigation methodology included

the technology investigation implementation included

the technology investigation direction was focused on

a supervised technology investigation was conducted

the technological investigation supervisor suggested

technological investigation research projects

technology investigation accomplishments

a technological investigation consultant

a technological investigation research lab

the technological investigation setting

a graduate technology investigation certificate was developed

the technology investigation deadlines

the leadership of the technology investigation included

the technological investigation research included

the results of the technological investigation

the focus of the technology investigation

the technology investigation applicants were asked to

the technology investigation faculty was formed to

there was enthusiasm about the technology investigation

a technological investigation specialist

the quality of the technological investigation

the success of the technological investigation

technological investigation planning

strategic technological investigation planning

yearly technological investigations

technology investigation facilities planning

technology investigation scheduling

instructional technological investigation

technological investigation participation

a progressive technological investigation

technology investigation planning experience

a successful technology investigation plan

the technology investigation operation plan

a technology investigation planning effort

the technology investigation planned program

technology investigation budget planning

the mission of the technology investigation

technology investigation exhibits

the organization planning of the technology investigation

the technology investigation oversight

the technology investigation was a planned experience

staff planned the technological investigation

the technological investigation planning skills

innovative techniques were used in the technological evaluation

a comprehensive technology investigation included

administrator input guided the technology investigation

technology investigation career planning

a dynamic technological investigation

technological investigation systems

technological investigation indicators

the priorities for the technology investigation

technological investigation process

early technology investigation planning

a structured technology investigation

an adjusted technology investigation

the technology investigation targets

a follow-up technology investigation plan

the technology investigation steps included

leadership for the technology investigation was used

technology investigation implementation

a technology investigation scheme

the features of the technology investigation

the technology investigation planned schedule

useful planning helped the technology investigation

the valuable planning paid off for the technology investigation

the amended technology investigation suggested

the technology investigation planning calendar was used to

the technology investigation had checkpoints

technology investigation research planning

technology investigation mistakes

the technology investigation vision

a subcommittee was formed for the technology investigation

technology investigation event planning was completed by

technology investigation unit planning

effective technology investigation planning

technology investigation duties

the objectives of the technological investigation were

a technological investigation planning portfolio

a potential technological investigation

technological investigation research decisions were based on

technological investigation requests

technology investigation planning ability

the role of the technological investigation

interest in the technological investigation

a managed technological investigation

the technology investigation planning format

the technology investigation cohort

technology investigation planning courses

it was an advanced technology investigation

planned technology investigation curriculum

technology investigation research activities

technology investigation expenses

it was an extended technology investigation

the technology investigation had significant findings

a technology investigation index was developed

there was specific planning for the technology investigation

there was mandatory training for technology investigation

the technology investigation was integrated with

an essential part of the technology investigation was

the technology investigation experience was challenging for

the technology investigation used surveys to collect

the technology investigation was put in understandable terms technology investigation development included

each technology investigation experiences centered on different aspects

the main strategy of the technology investigation was

a visionary contributed to the technology investigation

the technology investigation report usage was noted

rules were designed for the technology investigation

a technology investigation demonstration was designed for training

the terminology of the technology investigation

a technology investigation test was given to graduate students

the technology investigation was presented in a bilingual format

cues were given to the researchers using the technology investigation

the technical language was simplified in the technology investigation

probes were used in the technology investigation

the technology investigation had built in enrichment experiences

lessons were learned from the technology investigation

a suitable technology investigation was selected

support for the technology investigation was limited

the technology investigation had confusing prompts

support for the technology research investigation was difficult to obtain

the technological investigation was very detailed

the technological investigation was repetitive

the technological investigation was applicable to

it was a very specialized technology investigation

the technology investigation performance was analyzed

the technology investigation was put into context with

a guided approach was used with the technology investigation

it was an independent technology investigation

the main variables of the technology investigation included

the technology investigation was modeled after

solutions were sought for the technology investigation

technology investigation tasks were distributed to graduate students

the technological investigation focused on finding solutions

each specific problem was addressed in the technology investigation

there was a draft of the technology investigation

technology investigation tools were developed

technology investigation tasks were separated by

the focus of the technological investigation was twofold

a draft of the technology investigation was reviewed

a description of the technology investigation was

a narrative of the technology investigation found

technology investigations were divided into groups

errors were found in the technology investigation

the benefits of the technology investigation were massive

the technology investigation criteria included

the outcome of the technology investigation was positive

technology investigation reflection was encouraged

CHAPTER 6

TECHNOLOGICAL RESULTS PHRASES

technological development results

technological recruitment results

results of the technology sessions were included

technology accreditation results

results were presented to the technology consortium

advanced technology results were presented

technology scholars presented the results to

results of the technology program supported the

technology outreach results

results of the technology relations survey

technology accountability results

results of the technology skills surveys were analyzed

the technology needs results were discussed

results were analyzed with the technology goals

technology planning results

the results helped to plan the technology vision

the technology mission was reexamined after seeing the results

technology focus results

technology concerns were noted in the results

the technology implications and the results were reviewed by

the technology handbook contained the results section

technology reduction results

technology arbitrator results

a publication was made to present the technology results

technology results report

a technology statement was made based on the results

the results changed the technology requirements

a team reviewed the technology results

technology research results

suggestions were made from the technology results

technology results recommendations

opinions were expressed regarding the technology results

there were different views about the technology results

there were complaints about the technology results

the complaints of the technology results stemmed from

there was a debate about the technology results

technology presentation results

a questionnaire helped to focus the technology results

the technology results presentation was put on the schedule

teamwork was needed to compose the technology results

recognition was given for the high technology results

the technology proposal results indicated

organization was required to prepare the technology results

the technology experiment results included

the results of the technology experiment were published

the technology results were presented at a faculty meeting

technology results were used to provide enrichment for

results were presented for the technology candidates

technology training results indicated

there were some issues regarding the technology results

the technology results revealed competency issues

technology recommendation results

the technology results were reviewed

technology results changed some department experiences

technology performance results

practices were changed from the technology results

technology action results

technology review results

technology placement results

technology evaluation results

monitoring the technology results

the staff administration reviewed the technology results

a referral was made from the technology results

clearance was given for the technology results

new placement guidelines came from the technology results

technology record results

remarks were made about the technology results

the technology results were documented

the proceedings included a presentation of the technology results

the expectations of the technology results

the guidelines for the technology results helped to focus the

feedback was given on the technology results

informal feedback helped to explain the technology results

mistakes were made in calculating the technology results

the technology results were transferred to

technology follow-up results were presented

an image of the technology results was presented to

technology results revealed the quality of the program

the results of the technology assignment

compiling the technology results was demanding

the technology results changed the focus of the program

the researchers were interviewed about the technology results

technology checkpoint results

technology funding results

technology results were put in a clearinghouse

technology results were organized by

technology results were part of a collaboration

comments were made on the technology results

presenting the technology results took cooperation

technology term results

posting the technology results

the benefits of the technology results

technology results were divided into units

an agency examined the technology results

technology grant results

technology giving results

technology award results

project awards were established from the technology results

technology development results

results of the technology project revealed

there was some support for the technology results

technology relations results

technology gift results

technology assessment results

technology advancement results

technology institutional planning results

technology management results

technology program results

technology application results

the technology results were linked to

technology research grants results

the budget for the technology results was

technology annual funds results

technology corporate giving results

technology funding agency results

technology proposal development results

technology database results

technology private funding results

technology funding initiative results

technology telemarketing results

technology trust results

the foundation reviewed the technology results

the technology results showed the advancement of

the technology criteria and results revealed

the technology accountability results found

the procedure for presenting the technology results

advisement was needed for explaining the technology results

the technology results were encouraging

the technology results were re-analyzed

the technology results had complicated terminology

a research program reviewed the technology results

technology achievement results

the technology results contributed to

the technology results were used to develop standards

a statement of the technology results included

updated technology results

the technology results examined the strengths of the department

a record of the technology results found

computing the technology results was difficult

technology team performance results

technology division results

restructuring the technology results

technology advancement results

an inquiry was made into the technology results

results of the technology agreement

a partnership was developed from the technology agreement

a technology bulletin showcased the results of the study

the aim of presenting the technology results was to

the technology results were presented in context to

the intention of presenting the technology results was to

the technology results were seen in the realm of

the technology chairperson reviewed the results

the technology results were presented to the community

incentives were given for completing the technology results

technology results showed the accountability of the department

new methodology came from the technology results

technology competency results

team technology results were used to

peer reviews helped analyze the technology results

there were complaints about the technology results

cutbacks impacted the technology results

an authorization was needed to release the technology results

a faculty layoff effected the technology results

technology transfer results

a request was made from the chair to view the technology results

the technology results evaluated faculty salary

results included a technological interpretation

a faculty vacancy slowed down the completion of the technology results

faculty responses were included in the technology survey

an assistant was used to coordinate the technology results

stress was a factor in completing the technology results report

allocated technology results

technology standard results

self-directed technology results

technology supported results

self initiated technology results

technology results were presented objectively to

technology results were presented in alternative formats

technology clinical learning results

the results of the technology outcomes

multiage technology results were presented to

cooperative technology results indicated

technology service results

online technology learning results

the technology results were exemplary

problem based technology results

student centered technology results

integrated technology results

technology exploration results

technology module results

the technology results were one resource to

guided technology results

applicable technology results

technology results revealed mastery in

technology team focused results found

technology results profile

collective technology results

supplemental technology results

network technology results

instructional technology results

the implementation of the technology results was stifled by

procedures were developed to collect the technology results

technology unit results

technology software results

individualized technology results

program technology results

technology schedule results

technology intervention results

ongoing technology results

technology survey results found

thematic technology results

alternative instructional technology results

field based technology results

the success of the technology results collection was due to

the technology results impacted the future research designs

technology results were grouped by

instructional time impacted completing the technology results

numerous resources were used to collect the technology results

the initial technology results

CHAPTER 7

TECHNOLOGICAL RECOMMENDATION PHRASES

the most promising technology recommendation was

the estimated expenses for the technology recommendations were

the technology recommendations were misguided

researchers eagerly awaited the technology recommendations

business influenced the technology recommendations

the technology recommendations were made diligently

it was hard to support the technology recommendations

departments purchased the technology recommended equipment

departments were obligated to follow the technology recommendations

the technology recommendations were troublesome

one technology recommendation was very difficult to implement

parents were concerned about the technology recommendation

staff commented on the technology recommendations

the technology recommendations strained the

staff members felt overloaded from the technology recommendations

the technology recommendations opened the door for

there was a call for technology recommendations

the cost of the technology recommendations was calculated

only minor technological recommendations were made

an account was established for the technology recommendations

technology recommendations were listed in the

there was a schedule for presenting the technology recommendations

there was a logbook of technology recommendations

bids were reviewed for the technology recommendations

some technological recommendations were omitted

appointments were scheduled for technological recommendations

technology recommendations were put on hold

specialists lacked the skills to implement the technology recommendations

careful planning was made for the technology recommendations

technology recommendations were carried out by

the technology recommendations were ongoing

a management team worked on the technology recommendations

recommendations in the technology area were assigned case numbers

the administrators were watchful of the technology recommendations

a director was attentive to the technology recommendations

staff were apprehensive about some technology recommendations

staff were wasteful in implanting the technology recommendations

details were overlooked in the technology recommendations

extra equipment was needed for the technology recommendations

the team was delinquent in addressing the technology recommendations

processing funds delayed the technology recommendations

technology recommendations were reviewed meticulously

wasteful spending hindered the technology recommendations

the technology team reviewed the technology recommendations

some staff were indifferent about the technology recommendations

staff were cautious in making technology recommendations

the staff was noncommittal about the technology recommendations

technological recommendations were reviewed in the survey

a concern was pointed out in the technological recommendations

the technological recommendations originated from

researchers instigated the technological recommendations

the motive behind the technological recommendations included

technology recommendations were generated from

a timetable was developed for the technology recommendations

a focal point of the technology recommendations

at the center of the technology recommendations

the technology recommendations were indexed

definite recommendations were made in the technology area

the technology recommendations were complex

the technology recommendations were investigated

decisions were made regarding technology recommendations

technology recommendations were very detailed

the technology recommendations had stipulations

technology recommendations became controversial

allocations were made for the technology recommendations

the technology recommendations were defined

technology recommendations were categorized by

a list of technology recommendations was distributed to

the technology recommendations were made clear to

recommendations in the technology program were evident

improvements were made from the technology recommendations

the technology recommendations were included in

teachers collaborated on the technology recommendations

it took cooperation to make the technology recommendations

there was a unique combination of technology recommendations

information was imparted on the technology recommendations

an announcement was made on the technology recommendations

a complaint was made regarding the technology
recommendations

technology recommendations were completed by

the technology recommendations were perplexing

the most complicated technology recommendation was

reactions were mixed regarding the technology recommendations

it was apparent from the technology recommendations

there were compliments on the technology recommendations

concern was expressed regarding the technology
recommendations

the pending technology recommendations

some technology recommendations were restricted

security was an issue for the technology recommendations

there was turmoil regarding the technology recommendations

disorganization was a problem for the technology
recommendations

committees worked together on the technology recommendations

grants helped fund the technology recommendations

technology recommendations were made on a monthly basis

technology recommendations were consistent with

a constraint of the technology recommendations

conferences were developed to on technology recommendations

progress was made on the technology recommendations

the technology recommendations were called into question

more technology recommendations were expected

technology recommendations were demonstrated to

technology recommendations were combined with

technology recommendations resembled the

the criteria for the technology recommendations

the technology recommendations were critiqued

technology recommendations were judged on the basis of

the most influential technological recommendation was

technological recommendations made a big impact on

a specialist instructed the staff on the technology recommendations

a crew of consultants worked on the technology recommendations

technology recommendations opened up the

graduate students were unsure about the technology recommendations

students demanded help in learning the technology recommendations

comments were submitted on the technology recommendations

many faults were found in the technology recommendations

staff was pressured to make changes from the technology recommendations a significant factor in the technology recommendations

the technology recommendations were critical to the

a probe was made into the technology recommendations

technology recommendations were monitored weekly

documents supported the technology recommendations

controversy resulted from the technology recommendations

the technology recommendations were disputed

researchers were mislead by the technology recommendations

there were different opinions regarding the technology recommendations

a weakness of the technology recommendations

technology recommendations were justified by

consultants were straightforward about the technology recommendations

questions were answered on the technology recommendations

technology recommendations helped make important decisions

technology recommendations were delegated to

the purpose of the technology recommendations

technology recommendations are planned for

a yearly review of the technology recommendations

it was a well planned technology recommendation

proposed technology recommendations were displayed

the technology recommendations depend on

each department had technology recommendations

technology recommendations were described in

specifications were required for the technology recommendations

the technology recommendations were specialized

the final points of the technology recommendations include

new technology recommendations were discovered

in conclusion, the technology recommendations were

an elaborate technology recommendation was planned

technology recommendations were well managed

the technology recommendations had drawbacks

the technology recommendations were refined

the progress of the technology recommendations

technology recommendations were creative

technology recommendations were part of

technology recommendations were proposed

the technology recommendations were meaningful

the technology recommendations were disorganized

examples were given for the technology recommendations

technology recommendations helped the graduate students

technology recommendations were practical

the technology recommendations saved time

an effective technology recommendation was

efforts were made to change the technology recommendation

the staff brainstormed technology recommendations

the faculty had a new vision from the technology
recommendations

the technology recommendation brought

a new energy was created from the technology recommendations

the administration encouraged technology recommendations

students were engaged in the technology recommendations

technology recommendations were expanded to

eventually technological recommendations were

a team scrutinized the technological recommendations

an audit was conducted on the technological recommendations

technological recommendations are currently being expanded

technology recommendations were explained to

technology recommendations were confusing for

the technology recommendations were put in practical terms

the criticism of the technology recommendations

technology recommendations were unclear

technology recommendations were coherent

staff were reactionary to the technology recommendations

the technology recommendations were puzzling

a leading technology recommendation concerned

the technology recommendations were purposeful

scientific technology recommendations were made

the technology recommendation was deciphered

a rational technology recommendation was presented to

the technology recommendation was debatable

the technology recommendation had perplexing language

the technology recommendation was translated for

technology recommendation were presented to a diverse group

technology recommendations were geared to an urban setting

diverse language was used in the technology recommendations

ethnically diverse technology recommendations were presented

technology recommendations were impacted by political decisions

technology recommendations were presented in an international study

the technology recommendations surrounded an image of

technology recommendations emphasized recruitment

focused technology recommendations

technology recommendations surrounded choices

there was tension from the technology recommendations

an image was developed from the technology recommendations

inadequate support was given to the technology recommendations

there were limitations in the technology recommendations

options were given in the technology recommendations

future technology recommendations were

technology recommendations were confirmed by

progress resulted from the technology recommendations

the technology recommendations empowered the

the technology recommendations were recognized for

praise was given for the technology recommendations

a technology recommendation profile included

part of the technology recommendations were destructed

a discovery was made from the technology recommendations

an attribute of the technology recommendations

philosophical technology recommendations were confusing

understandable and practical technology recommendations were

security was an issue in the technology recommendations

an enhancement was made in the technology recommendations

credit was given for developing the technology recommendations

CHAPTER 8

TECHNOLOGICAL CHANGE PHRASES

technological change is essential for

there are unlimited opportunities with technological change

changing technology benefits society by

one approach to changing technology is

an academic approach to changing technology

changing technology must address the

investigating technological changes requires

a report on technological change was presented to

some teachers were critics of the changing technology

the college acknowledged that the technology was changing

the chair approved the technological change

the changing technology was not accepted by the team

changing technology created new problems for

technology changes were negotiated by

a team of professors reviewed the technology changes

funding had an impact on the technological changes

adjustments were made for the changing technology

changes were approved in the technology area

questions were posed about the changing technology

problems were resolved concerning the changing technology

a limitation of the changing technology was

changing technology created new avenues for

technological changes were presented to

each division had technological changes

the board adopted the technology changes

clearance was granted for the technology changes

the staff needed training for the technology changes

action was taken to address the technology changes

reaction was mixed for the changing technology

the changing technology was functional for

there were delays with the changing technology

priority was given for the technological changes

the changing technology interfered with

the specific technological changes were reviewed

the staff defined the technological changes

each technological change required approval

a plan was developed to address technology changes

a lecture was given on changing technology

the pros and cons of changing technology were discussed

committees were formed to discuss the changing technology

the administration questioned the technological changes

technological changes were aligned with

specialists formed the objectives for the technology changes

instruction improved from the technology changes

technological changes were coordinated with

adjustments in the changing technology helped

technological changes were adopted by

the changing technology was utilized to

the research board applauded the technology changes

the advantages of the changing technology

staff training was provided for the technology changes

consultants helped implement the technology changes

a guide was written on the technology changes

a task force advocated the changing technology

the changing technology influenced the

encouragement was needed for the technology changes

additional instruction was given on the changing technology

faculty were anxious about the changing technology

the changing technology alarmed for staff

in-service training was conducted on the technology changes

the aim of the changing technology was to

the technological changes coincided with

the technology changes were completed ahead of schedule

compromises were made in the technology changes

the proposed technological changes

a rigid schedule was developed to complete the technology
changes

technological change was accelerated

there were consequences of the technology changes

many details were addressed in the technology changes

specialized skills were required for the technology changes

mistakes were made as the technological changes took place

a detailed account explained the technology changes

technology changes were completed by

each technology change was negotiated

problems were resolved with the new technology changes

technology changes were finished on schedule

the technology changes went unquestioned

information was gathered on the technology changes

the technology changes were authorized by

changes in technology were initiated by

there were some negative reactions to the technology changes

a response was made regarding the technology changes

faculty took part in the technology changes

a grant covered the cost of the technology changes

a proposal stating the technological changes was submitted

a formal announcement was made about the technology changes

there were hurdles with the technology changes

questions were presented on the technology changes

technology changes were added to

an extension was made for additional technology changes

the faculty made compromises for the technology changes

a new division was created to address the technology changes

changes advanced the technology program

progress was made on the technological changes

the administration promoted the technology changes

a timeline helped organize the technological changes

headway was made with the technological changes

technology changes enriched the research department

technology changes provided more research opportunities

the department was recognized for the technology changes

the technology changes set a precedent

the technology changes provided a new direction for

technology changes were communicated through

technology changes were circulated

technology changes were posted in the

recommendations were made from the technology changes

each technology change was reviewed

technology staff were given directives from the changes

financial problems impacted the technology changes

a committee opposed the technological changes

an agency was consulted in making the technological changes

technology changes were addressed promptly

changes were proposed in the technology agreements

technology changes corresponded with

technological changes were made earlier than expected

technology changes were completed at different stages

a group of faculty recommended the technology changes

the technology changes required many revisions

there were several options in making the technology changes

a technological change committee modified the

new technology changes were suggested

faculty received notification of the technology changes

there were many technology change decisions

the board favored the technology changes

the technology changes were visible

appropriate technology changes were made

arguments were presented on the changing technology

each technological change was challenged

technological changes encompassed

arrangements were made on the changing technology

the technology changes were perplexing

the purpose of the technology changes was to

some aspects of the technological changes were questioned

the technology changes were made in cooperation with

staff became familiar with the technology changes

the cost of the technology changes was calculated

the staff collected surveys on technological change

consultants were invited to speak on changing technology

there were automated technology changes

the technological changes were feasible

changes in the technology department were sidetracked

each department advocated for technology changes

departments were asked to make technological changes

staff did not have the background to make technology changes

the district was prompted to make technology changes

technological changes strengthened the

the division moved forward with the technology changes

changes in the technology program were defective

careless mistakes were made in changing the technology

a stumbling block in changing the technology was

there were many barriers in changing the technology

the change in technology was based on

a restriction for changing the technology

technology centers changed location

a change in technology hindered

specialists struggled with the technology changes

technological changes continued to occur

there was pressure to make technological changes

the benefit of the changing technology was to

each college instituted technology changes

some faculty did not support the technological changes

technological changes created problems in the areas of

the technology changes were launched quickly

technology changes were made on behalf of

poor judgments impacted the technology changes

there were some suspicions about the changing technology

there were various opinions about the technology changes

conclusions were made concerning the changing technology

management addressed the technological changes

students had trouble adapting the new technology changes

it took a long time to put technological changes in motion

the routine changed with the new technology

new goals were formed from the changing technology

technological changes were made at different intervals

there were guidelines to adhere to the changing technology

the challenge of the technological changes

the technology changes were unpopular

some of the technology changes were unreasonable

a chart was made of the technology changes

equipment was borrowed to make the technology changes

technology changes required an equipment inventory

some of the technology changes malfunctioned

a failure of the technology changes was the

each technology change caused

a small percent of students agreed with the technology changes

technology changes received a positive perception from

insightful technology changes were made

a technology change newsletter was developed

technology changes were placed on the website

social media was used to promote the technology changes

technology changes were petitioned

the philosophy of the technology changes was described by

technology changes were formatted to

the technology changes were piloted by the

research mini grants emphasized technology change

the technology changes were used in research projects

the community supported the technology changes

viewpoints were varied on technology change

comments were negative about the technology changes

technology changes were made in small steps

technology changes impacted the image of the university

the technology changes were altered for the

technology changes effected the department regulations

the pace of technological change was fast

technology change guidelines involved

a change in technology meant department changes

graduate students spoke out about the technology changes

technology changes were uncomfortable for some people

graduate school support was given for the technology changes

technological changes modified class assignments

network support helped the technology changes

the dissertation was on technology change in the department

more research projects were on the topic of technology change

the basic idea behind the technology change was

one important technology change came from

technology changes were important for future decisions

no technology changes were made this year

future technology changes will be explore

RECOMMENDED READING

Peterson, S. (2015). *Digital Research Phrase Book*

The ***Digital Research Phrase Book*** contains thousands of research phrases from a digital and electronic perspective. Many phrases in research reports and papers often have a technological or computer type of focus. The book lists phrases and examines developing ideas and phrases from a virtual perspective of looking into network relationships, electronic features, technology aspects, online data collection and various cyber elements that connect the research and testing world.

Peterson, S. (March 22, 2013-Kindle Version). *The Research Writer's Phrase Book: A guide to proposal writing and research phraseology.* **Lanham, MD: International Scholars Publications.**

*The Research Writer's Phrase Book (*available in both Kindle and print versions) helps guide research writers in the writing process as they start to develop research proposals and written research projects. The book contains research phrases on topics such as the purpose, objectives, need for the study, review of literature, methodology, conclusions, recommendations and implications for the study.

Peterson, S, (1998). *The Educators' Phrase Book: A complete reference guide.* **Bethesda, MD: International Scholars Publications.**

The Educators' Phrase Book: A complete reference guide is a book that contains phrases to help educators in their writing efforts. Some of the phrases cover topics related to curriculum, behavior, instructional and learning phrases, school planning and assessment, as well as teacher, principal and student phrases.

INDEX

Content, 13-14

Core, 7

Criteria, 10, 67

Curriculum, 5, 8

D

Decision (s), 7

Demonstration, 19

Design, 6

Discussion, 18

Dissertation, 80

Draft, 4,11, 60

E

Example, 9

Endorsement, 3

Endowment, 3

Extension, 5

Evaluation, 1, 6, 25-36

Evidence, 5

Exhibit, 19

F

Faculty, 50, 58, 69, 90, 93

Feedback, 65

Focus, 1-12

Foundation (s), 3, 7

M

Management, 2, 66

Method (s), 23, 51

Mentor (s), 4

Mission, 1, 51, 62

Model, 15, 18, 33

N

Newsletter, 21

O

Objective(s), 2, 13-23

Organization (s), 22,50

Orientation, 15, 23

Outcomes, 2,11,17,21

Outreach, 7

Overview, 6,43

P

Partnership, 50

Peer review, 69

Performance, 21, 36,53

Plan, 1,9

Policy, 2, 36, 38, 43-48

Portfolio, 37

Practicum, 17

T

U

V

W

Y

AFTERWORD

As an experienced academic writer I have developed articles and grant proposals for years before the technological surge started to enter the academic world. This rapid changing technology has forced many professionals to rethink how academic writings are phrased and have shifted many of their writings to have more of a technical and digital focus. The ***Tech Research Phrase Book*** is a wonderful department, library and campus resource for anyone interested in academic writing with a technological shift in style. This wonderful association between technology and writing can be started by a phrase or two to spur this writing connection. Each writing project will have a unique focus so the phrases can be a good starting point to explore how a personal technology project can be incorporated with the written formants that are used to develop ideas, concepts and future projects.

www.ingramcontent.com/pod-product-compliance
Lightning Source LLC
Chambersburg PA
CBHW031308060726

47590CB00003B/1104